917.
9447
WUE

Wuerthner, George.

Yosemite.

WITHDRAWN

DATE			

"No temple made with hands can compare with Yosemite. Every rock in its walls seems to glow with life." —John Muir

Yosemite

The Grace & Grandeur

George Wuerthner

Voyageur Press | *Discovery* A Pictorial Guide

On the frontispiece:
Half Dome overlooks the
Merced River.

On the title page:
The sunset glows on a ponderosa pine forest along the rim of
the Merced River Canyon.

On the facing page:
El Capitan towers 3,000 feet
above the Merced.

On the contents page:
Ragweed frames Yosemite Falls,
which has dwindled to a trickle
in late summer.

Edited by Amy Rost-Holtz
Designed by Maria Friedrich
Printed in Hong Kong

02 03 04 05 06   5 4 3 2 1

Library of Congress Cataloging-in-Publication Data
Wuerthner, George.
  Yosemite : the grace & grandeur / George Wuerthner.
    p. cm. — (A pictorial discovery guide)
Includes bibliographical references and index.
  ISBN 0-89658-487-9
  1. Yosemite National Park (Calif.)—Pictorial works. 2. Yosemite National Park (Calif.)—Description and travel. I. Title. II. Series.
F868.Y6 W84 2002
979.4'47—dc21
                                        2002001883

Distributed in Canada by Raincoast Books, 9050 Shaughnessy Street, Vancouver, B.C. V6P 6E5

Published by Voyageur Press, Inc.
123 North Second Street, P.O. Box 338, Stillwater, MN 55082 U.S.A.
651-430-2210, fax 651-430-2211
books@voyageurpress.com
www.voyageurpress.com

Contents

Introduction 9

Below the Valley: 41
Southern Yosemite

The Incomparable
Yosemite Valley 53

The High Country: 95
Tuolumne Meadows and Beyond

Bibliography 140

Index 142

Map of Yosemite National Park 143

About the Author 144

Introduction

I first visited the Yosemite Valley when I was nineteen years old. I hitchhiked from Montana to California and entered the east side of the park at Tioga Pass. I arrived in Tuolumne Meadows just before dusk and set off immediately for a back-country campsite. I reached Upper Cathedral Lake just as the last light of the day lit the white granite monolith of 10,991-foot Cathedral Peak to a burnish pink. The trail to the lake was still blocked in places by lingering snow patches, and the lake was partially frozen. Yet some open water reflected the peaks and sky, providing an unbelievable first impression of the beauty of Sierra Nevada granite. I threw my sleeping bag out on a rocky bench near the lake. With a multitude of stars above and Yosemite granite below, I quickly fell asleep.

In the morning, I found a trail sign pointing to the Yosemite Valley. I didn't have a map and decided to follow the river downhill, figuring it would end up in the Yosemite Valley at some point. Climbing across slabs of granite, down steep glacier-carved rocky steps, I quickly dropped in elevation, leaving behind the snowfields.

That first morning's hike left me with two indelible impressions of Yosemite. First, Yosemite is a world of rock. There is bedrock exposed everywhere—bedrock slabs, bedrock domes, bedrock cliffs, and bedrock ledges. Sometimes there are boulder erratics, left by retreating glaciers, resting on the bedrock. There are places where the glaciers have worn the rock surface as smooth as a marble tabletop. This rock is a hard, firm granite nearly as white as the lingering snow patches. It has a dazzling purity that seems to glow from within.

The second thing that caught my eyes and ears was falling water. With snowfields melting under the summer sun, water is nearly as abundant the rock. Water seems to seep, dash, and run from every crack and ledge. It pours off cliffs. It slides across slabs. It tumbles down boulder fields. It gathers into swirls, eddies, and rills that run together to form ever larger streams, which then thunder into gorges and fall into the Yosemite Valley.

Despite the lengthy introduction to the park's wonders that the hike provided, I simply wasn't prepared for the incredible beauty of the valley. When I walked into the upper valley and beheld Yosemite Falls, Half Dome, El Capitan, the limpid green waters of the Merced River, and the spacious meadows, it was almost more than I could register. It was a visual sensory overload. There are, of course, other places with lovely rivers, beautiful forests, spectacular cliffs and waterfalls. But no single place brings them together in such a perfect union as Yosemite. I have visited Yosemite countless times since that first introduction, but I never tire of the valley's changing views.

Previous page:

In the lower part of the Yosemite Valley, the waters of the Merced run clear and calm.

Facing page:

Glaciers carved the Yosemite landscape. As they moved along, glaciers plucked rocks up from one place, then as they melted left them elsewhere. Rocks such as these, called erratics, now lie on the bedrock along the headwaters of Lewis Creek.

The Best of the Best

As perfect as Yosemite is, it is part of a much larger piece of real estate that is equally as impressive. The park is 150 miles east of San Francisco on the western slope of the Sierra Nevada—one of the truly great mountain ranges on earth. Encompassing more than 20 million acres, the range's area equals that of Maine. More than 400 miles long, it is also the longest continuous range in the lower forty-eight states and one of the longest barriers to roads in the country. The second largest roadless area in the lower forty-eight states is found here; from Tioga Pass, it is 150 miles south to Walker Pass without a single road. Kings Canyon, more than 8,000 feet in depth, is considered by some to be the deepest in the United States. Thirteen peaks in the Sierra exceed 14,000 feet, including Mount Whitney, the highest point in the lower forty-eight states.

Despite its lofty heights, this spectacular landscape is blessed with what some have said is the sunniest and mildest climate of any major mountain range in the world. Summers are dominated by day after day of nearly cloudless sky. Temperatures in the Yosemite Valley are moderate with cool nights, and higher elevations may be frosty. Autumn is crisp but clear, with warm days and pleasantly cool nights. Winter is seldom harsh; sub-zero temperatures are rare. And even snowfall, though abundant and frequent, is interrupted by periods of sunny weather.

Within what is a superlative mountain range, Yosemite stands out as the best of the best, and within the park borders are the some of the grandest scenic spectacles in the world.

The borders of Yosemite National Park encompass the headwaters of the Tuolumne River and Merced River, an area of 761,266 acres. Its elevations range from 2,000 feet in the lower Merced River Gorge to 13,114 feet on top of Mount Lyell. The park is surrounded by lands managed by the U.S. Forest Service, including the Stanislaus, Toiyabe, Inyo, and Sierra National Forests.

The Merced River drops over Vernal Fall. This waterfall, like many others in the park, tumbles from a hanging valley left by Ice Age glaciers.

A replica of a typical Indian hut can be seen behind the main visitor center in the Yosemite Valley. Though native people roamed throughout the Sierra Nevada, their primary villages were located in the foothills and Central Valley. A small group of people also once resided in the Yosemite Valley.

Yosemite History

The best documentation suggests that people permanently occupied what is now Yosemite National Park within only the last 1,200 years. These people, known as the Miwok, were only one of thirteen tribal affiliations that inhabited the Sierra Nevada at the time of first European contact. Native settlements were scattered throughout the valley. Most of the larger permanent villages had a few hundred residents. From these villages, smaller seasonal camps were established in seasonal hunting or food gathering locations. Due to snow and cold weather, most habitation occurred below 4,000 feet. Though no permanent villages were located at higher elevations, native peoples regularly traveled across the Sierra Nevada to trade.

Throughout the Sierra Nevada, human population was concentrated in a few favored locations, primarily along the larger streams and rivers from the Central Valley. Many areas of the Sierra Nevada were seldom visited except for small bands of roving hunters.

The exact number of inhabitants that once resided in the Yosemite area is difficult to estimate. Recent attempts suggest that as many as 55,000 people may have lived on both sides of the range, including the Central Valley adjacent to the foothills, but probably no more than few hundred people ever permanently lived in what now is Yosemite National Park.

European Exploration of the Sierra Nevada

In 1772, a Spanish padre, who spied the snowy mountains from the Sacramento River delta, was the first to describe the Sierra Nevada range in a written account. By this same time, French trappers were penetrating the Rocky Mountains from the east, yet the Sierra Nevada less than 200 miles from the Pacific Ocean was unknown. In 1776, another missionary, Pedro Font, beheld the mountains from near San Francisco Bay and named them the Sierra Nevada, or snow-covered range. The name stuck, but it wasn't until 1806—the same year that the Lewis and Clark expedition completed its momentous trek across the entire West—that Spanish explorers even penetrated the Sierra Nevada foothills. In that year, an expedition under the command of Gabriel Moraga left San Francisco, crossed the San Joaquin Valley, then traveled south along the foot of the range to the Kern River. Along the way Morago crossed and named the Rio de Nuestra Senora de la Merced—what today is known as Merced River.

The next European to encounter the Sierra Nevada was the intrepid mountain man Jedediah Smith, for whom the Smith River and Jedediah Smith Redwoods State Park in northern California are named. In 1826, he left Wyoming with a party of trappers and crossed Utah, Nevada, and the Mojave Desert to enter southern California. After visiting the San Gabriel Mission near present-day Los Angeles, Smith's party traveled north up the San Joaquin Valley searching for a way to cross the Sierra Nevada. Leaving the rest of the party camped in the Sierra foothills, Smith and two others succeeded in crossing the range near Ebbetts Pass just north of present-day Yosemite National Park. Smith and his companions were the first whites to actually penetrate and cross the range.

In 1833, another trapping party of seventy men under the command of Joseph Walker (for whom Walker Pass and the Walker River are named) crossed the Sierra Nevada through what is now Yosemite National Park. They traveled the divide between the Merced and Tuolumne drainages, likely following closely what is today the Tioga Pass road. As the party floundered about in the snowy mountains, Walker's clerk Zenas Leonard noted that they encountered "small streams which would shoot out from under these high snow-banks, and after running a short distance in deep chasms which they have through ages cut in the rocks, precipitate themselves from one lofty precipice to another, until they are exhausted in rain below. Some of these precipices appeared to us to be more than a mile high." Most historians believe Leonard was describing the streams descending the northern shoulder of the Yosemite Valley.

A few days later Leonard noted in his journal that the party traveled through "trees of the Redwood species, incredibly large—some of which would measure 16–18 fathoms round the trunk at the height of a man's

Winter snow lies deep in the Mariposa Grove of Giant Sequoias. Sequoia trees have a limited distribution in the Sierra Nevada. Three major groves—the Merced, Tuolumne, and Mariposa—are found in Yosemite National Park.

head from the ground." His descriptions can leave no doubt that the Walker Party passed through the Tuolumne grove of sequoia, making them the first Europeans to view the wonders of the Yosemite Valley and describe the giant trees.

The Gold Rush and Indian Wars

Mountain men trapped in many of the foothill streams of the Sierra Nevada, but few, if any, trapped very far up the drainages into the mountains. The Yosemite Valley remained unknown to anyone but a small number of Native American inhabitants and adventurous Europeans. All this changed in 1848. On a January morning along the American River near present-day Sacramento, James Marshall plucked a nugget of gold from John Sutter's sawmill raceway, starting one of the largest mass migrations in American history—the California Gold Rush. The number of Americans in the area swelled from 2,000 to more than 53,000 within a year. By 1850, several hundred thousand people had flooded into California.

Fanning out across the Sierra foothills, they quickly discovered that placer gold was common in river gravel from the Feather and Yuba Rivers in the north to the Tuolumne and Merced Rivers in the south. Some miners followed these gold deposits upstream until they discovered the Mother Lode or source vein for the stream-deposited gold. Two such men, William Abrams and U. N. Reamer, were hunting for a potential mill site along the Merced River when they came upon an Indian trail that lead to "stupendous cliffs rising perhaps 3,000 feet from their base and which gave us cause for wonder. Not far off a waterfall dropped from a cliff below three jagged peaks into the valley, while farther beyond a rounded mountain stood, the valley side of which looked as though it had been sliced with a knife as one would slice a loaf of bread and which Reamer and I called the Rock of Ages." To anyone familiar with the area, the description could refer only to Half Dome and the Yosemite Valley.

Abrams and Reamer did not promote their discovery, so the trails to Yosemite remained obscure for another few years. But the continued influx of miners set up growing conflicts with the native people and ultimately precipitated more exploration of the remote reaches of the mountains.

In their mad dash for gold, miners swarmed over the mountains, displacing Indians from their village sites and destroying their food sources. The Indians retaliated by raiding the miners' camps, taking food, and sometimes killing individuals.

In 1850, a group of Indians were alleged to have robbed and then killed several white traders at a trading post in Coursegold. In response, a volunteer militia, called the Mariposa Battalion, was created to scour the mountains to round up the marauding bands of Indians and place them on a reservation.

The militia traveled up the South Fork of the Merced to present-day Wawona. With members of the "Yosemite" band of Indians as guides, the militia was led to the band's settlement in the valley by following roughly the route of today's highway from Wawona to the Yosemite Valley. Near Old Inspiration Point, the group was treated to the full view of the valley. One member of the militia, Lafayette Bunnell, described the scene: "The grandeur of the scene was softened by the haze that hung over the valley—light as gossamer—and by the clouds which partially dimmed the higher cliffs and mountains. This obscurity of vision but increased the awe with which I beheld it, and as I looked, a peculiar exalted sensation seemed to fill my whole being, and I found my eyes in tears with emotions." The members of Bunnell's group were the first Europeans known to have both seen and visited Half Dome, Vernal and Nevada Falls, Mirror Lake, and other well-known sights.

By May, the militia, under the command of Captain John Boling (spelled Bowling in some accounts), was back again in the Yosemite Val-

ley, capturing Chief Teneiya, leader of the Yosemite band of Indians. With Teneiya as guide, Boling and some of his men climbed out of the valley and explored as far as the Mount Hoffmann region. The next day they went up Tenaya Creek, then Snow Creek towards Tenaya Lake, which Boling named for the chief.

Tourism Comes to the Valley

The first tourists arrived in 1855. James Mason Hutchings, a young Englishman and former gold-rush miner, along with artist Thomas Ayres and several other companions, were guided into the valley by two Indians. They spent five days marveling at the scenery. The following summer, Hutchings launched a new publication, *Hutchings' California Magazine*, designed to promote the state and its attributes to an eager public throughout the country and world. Many of the articles in the magazine extolled the majesty of the Yosemite Valley. In 1860, Hutchings published the first guidebook to the Yosemite area.

Other publicists were soon journeying to the valley. The Reverend Thomas Starr King (for whom Mount Starr King is named), a pastor from New England, visited the valley and wrote a glowing account for a Boston paper. King suggested that the beauty of Yosemite exceeded even the best canyons of the Alps and Andes. C. L. Weed and C. E. Watkins

Above:

Tenaya Lake was one of the first park features named by Europeans. Lafayette Bunnell of the Mariposa Battalion named the lake in 1851 for Teneiya, chief of the Native Americans who lived in the Yosemite Valley.

Facing Page:

Lying between the upper Merced River and Tenaya Creek, Half Dome is perhaps the most remarkable feature in a remarkable valley. As its name implies, the mountain appears to have been split in two with one side rounded into a dome, while the other is a sheer cliff 2,500 feet tall.

both made early photographs of the valley that were published, among other places, in *Hutchings' California Magazine*. Albert Bierstadt, a well-known landscape painter of the era, produced grand paintings of the valley and falls, further adding to the public's curiosity and desire to visit the region.

The first rustic accommodations were built by 1857, and by 1859, the Upper Hotel was constructed. Hutchings purchased the hotel in 1863, then moved permanently to the valley. He and others also started to "claim" squatter's rights to the valley.

Yosemite Becomes a Park

By 1864, the growing throng of tourists visiting the Yosemite area grabbed the attention of Israel Ward Raymond, the California representative of the Central American Steamship Transit Company. Interested in promoting tourism, while at the same time preventing unbridled privatization of the valley, Raymond sent a letter to U.S. Senator John Conness (for whom Mount Conness is named), urging preservation of the valley and nearby sequoia trees. To bolster his request, Raymond argued that the surrounding mountains with their large tracts of bare granite were useless for timber production.

Conness soon introduced legislation into Congress to protect the Yosemite Valley and several sequoia groves as a park under the administration of the state of California. President Abraham Lincoln signed the bill into law on June 30, 1864. (It is important to note that the bill Lincoln signed didn't create a national park, but transferred federal lands to the care of California for use as a state park. Although a park in the Yosemite Valley was established eight years prior to the creation of Yellowstone National Park in Wyoming, Yellowstone is still considered the world's first national park.) The bill signaled a change in the American policy of giving away federal lands for development and was one of the first attempts in the country to protect a natural area for future generations.

The creation of the park also set up one of the first property rights issues faced in the nation's fledgling attempts at conservation. Hutchings and others had "claimed" land in the valley but had never secured legal title to it. Technically they had no legal authority to the land, but by right of occupancy they tried to secure title to it. They took their cause to the California legislature and ultimately to the U.S. Congress.

The U.S. Senate noted that the men had no legal title to the lands they claimed and, in the case of Hutchings, had only settled in the valley two months prior to the passage of the legislation creating the park. The Senate reasoned that the land within the Yosemite Valley had been given to the state to protect, and California had an obligation to keep it in public ownership. Congress, upholding the ideal of public control of spe-

cial natural areas, rejected the men's claims. Hutchings took his suit to the U.S. Supreme Court but lost there as well.

Though they had no legal claim to the lands, Hutchings and the other squatters enjoyed public sympathy in California, and they were richly rewarded when the California legislature voted to reimburse them. Though he lost claim to acreage in the valley, Hutchings maintained a cabin there until his death in 1902.

The fact that Congress and the courts upheld the challenge to the park and public control of natural landscapes reinforced the public policy shift that began with the creation of the park in 1864. The protection of Yosemite as a park set the stage for our entire system of national parks, forests, wildlife refuges, and other federal land holdings.

John Muir, founder of the Sierra Club and one of the best-known spokespersons for the creation of Yosemite National Park, found his inspiration and his life's work while wandering Yosemite's canyons and peaks. (Library of Congress, LC-USZ62-52000)

John Muir, Apostle for Preservation

No name is more intertwined with Yosemite and the Sierra Nevada than John Muir. He is commemorated by place names throughout the wide West he rambled: Muir Pass in Kings Canyon National Park, Camp Muir on Mount Rainier, Muir Inlet and Muir Glacier in Glacier Bay National Park, Mount Muir in Prince William Sound, Muir Woods National Monument by San Francisco, Muir Gorge in Yosemite, and the John Muir Trail, which traverses the highest parts of the Sierra Nevada. Yet Muir left more than his name upon the map, for he was and still is a central figure in the environmental movement.

Muir wrote numerous articles and a book extolling the beauty of

Yosemite. He urged people to get to know the mountains first hand and to always preserve and protect the wildlands from unwise development. He was largely responsible for the creation of Yosemite National Park, plus he helped to raise public awareness of several other areas that eventually became parks, including the Grand Canyon in Arizona and Glacier Bay in Alaska.

Muir is one of the most visionary wildlands supporters that ever lived. He had a religious fervor for wilderness that supported him throughout his long life. His holistic perception of nature is viewed as radical even by some of today's conservation standards.

After briefly visiting Yosemite in 1868, Muir took a job in 1869 supervising a sheepherder and flock of sheep bound for the Yosemite high country. The arrangement he had with the rancher allowed him to explore the surrounding country.

After a summer with the sheep, Muir took a job as a sawmill operator with James Hutchings. Cutting only downed timber, Muir worked on and off for Hutchings, with ample time to saunter through the valley observing and enjoying the natural world around him. After leaving Hutchings' employment, Muir remained in the valley, eking out a living guiding tourists, which gave him more time to explore.

Visitors were struck with Muir's intensity of purpose and his unending praise for Yosemite and the mountains. In ragged, ill-fitting clothes, he looked every bit the vagabond, but he spoke with the intelligence and style of a well-educated gentleman. Joseph Leconte, a professor at the University of California, Berkeley, encountered Muir in 1871 while on a field trip with some students. Leconte was a geologist, and during his rambles with Muir, they discussed Muir's theories for the geological origins of the Yosemite landscape. Muir had begun to look at the glacier history of the region, tracing the path of former glaciers, even discovering some relict Sierran glaciers. He was convinced that glaciers had shaped and honed the Yosemite landscape. (Josiah Whitney, the leading geologist of the time, proposed that a cataclysmic earthquake had suddenly created the valley.) Leconte was among a growing legion of fans who helped to increase Muir's fame and reputation among academics.

Clinton Merriam, a New York Congressman, also visited Muir in 1871. After Muir expounded his glacial theories to Merriam, the Congressman urged him to send an article to the *New York Tribune*. Muir was more than a little surprised when his article "Yosemite Glaciers" was accepted and published. He was soon publishing his glacial articles in other venues, including the *American Journal of Science* and *Proceedings of the American Association for the Advancement of Science*.

In 1874, Muir moved to San Francisco and settled into a more civilized life. He wrote more articles about the Sierra, growing in fame, if not fortune. He continued to demonstrate a true ecological, holistic understanding of nature and advocated for the protection of entire landscapes.

Hikers walk along the John Muir Trail, which links Yosemite with Mount Whitney and traverses the highest parts of the Sierra Nevada. Muir is commemorated by place names throughout the wide West he rambled.

In an 1890 article for *Century Magazine*, he wrote: "For the branching canons and valleys of the basins of the streams that pour into Yosemite are as closely related to it as are the fingers to the palm of the hand—as the branches, foliage, and flowers of a tree to the trunk. Therefore, very naturally, all the fountain region above Yosemite, with its peaks, canons, snowfields, glaciers, forests, and streams, should be included in the park to make it an harmonious unit instead of a fragment, great though the fragment be; while to the westward, below the valley, the boundary might be extended with great advantage far enough to comprehend the Fresno, Mariposa, Merced, and Tuolumne groves of big trees, three of which are on roads leading to the valley, while all of them in the midst of conifers scarcely less interesting than the colossal brown giants themselves."

Muir's articles helped persuade Congress to pass legislation in 1890 creating Yosemite National Park, which included the headwaters of the Tuolumne and Merced but not the state-controlled Yosemite Valley.

This successful Yosemite campaign launched Muir's career as an environmental activist. In 1892, Muir, with a number of other like-minded individuals, formed the Sierra Club in San Francisco. With Muir as its president, the Sierra Club lobbied for greater protection of forested lands and new national parks. Muir increasingly became a spokesperson for the fledging environmental movement.

In this historical photo of Hetch Hetchy before the Tuolumne River was dammed, it is easy to see why John Muir considered this valley the scenic twin of the Yosemite Valley and argued that it was too spectacular to be used as a reservoir site. After losing the battle for Hetch Hetchy, Muir mourned its loss under the reservoir, which still covers the valley today. (Historical photo courtesy of the Yosemite Museum, Yosemite National Park)

Federal Protection

In 1891, Congress amended an existing land law to allow the president to create forest reserves in the West. President Benjamin Harrison promptly created fifteen forest reserves, including one that took in four million acres along the Sierra crest. The reserves were much like most of today's national parks in their management—no grazing or logging was permitted. President Grover Cleveland created thirteen new forest reserves in 1897.

The job of protection became easier when Vice President Theodore Roosevelt assumed the presidency in 1901. Founder of the Boone and Crockett Club, Roosevelt was an amateur naturalist, an excellent birder, a passionate hunter, and one of the most conservation-minded presidents ever to hold the office. During his term, he greatly expanded the national forest system and created sixteen national monuments, fifty-three wildlife reserves, and five new national parks. With such a strong, mutual interest in nature, it was only natural that Muir and Roosevelt should meet. During a 1903 visit to California, Roosevelt contacted Muir and arranged to accompany him on a wilderness tour.

Muir persuaded Roosevelt to extend forest reserve protection for the rest of the Sierra Nevada north of Yosemite all the way to Mount Shasta. Disgusted as much as Muir with the shabby commercialization of the valley that had been permitted under state control, Roosevelt agreed that the valley would be better off in federal hands. He encouraged Muir to work towards persuading the California state legislature to cede the state park surrounding the Yosemite Valley to the federal government.

In 1905, the Yosemite Valley and the Mariposa Grove were placed back under federal control.

The Battle over Hetch Hetchy

With the transfer of Yosemite Valley to federal ownership and its incorporation into Yosemite National Park, Muir thought Yosemite was finally protected from further desecration. But the effort to protect the park was just starting. Unknown to Muir and the Sierra Club and without much fanfare, Congress passed a bill in 1901 that allowed water conduits to pass through national parks. Immediately, the city of San Francisco filed for rights to construct a dam and reservoir in the Hetch Hetchy Canyon along the Tuolumne River within Yosemite National Park.

The Sierra Club opposed the dam, and Muir was soon writing articles defending the valley. He pointed out that there had been little public discussion, and furthermore, there were many other potential water sources that could satisfy San Francisco's needs without damming Hetch Hetchy.

In a battle that spanned twelve years, Muir and other Yosemite supporters campaigned nationally to elicit popular support for protecting

the valley from development, while at the same time lobbying the president and Congress. Many nationally prominent figures including William Brewster, William Hornady, Ernest Thompson Seton, George Bird Grinnell, and Frederick Law Olmsted Jr., joined Muir in condemning the Hetch Hetchy project. Finally, after Woodrow Wilson assumed the presidency in 1913, Congress passed a bill allowing the dam construction in Hetch Hetchy to begin. Frail and worn out, and some say heartbroken over the loss of Hetch Hetchy, Muir died of pneumonia less than a year later.

However, one positive aftermath of the Hetch Hetchy controversy was the creation of the National Park Service, which gave national parks a new unity and purpose. (Until its establishment 1916, the parks had no central authority, and each was more or less run as a separate entity.)

Other Threats

The battle to preserve Hetch Hetchy Canyon may be the best-known attack on Yosemite's ecological integrity, but it was not the only one. Almost as soon as the park was established, there were calls to adjust its boundaries to permit logging of its large sugar pines or to open other sections to mining or livestock grazing.

When the park was first designated, there was no agency to manage it. Instead, the U.S. Army was given authority for patrolling the park. Given the limited force they had and the remote nature of much of Yosemite at the time, the army found it difficult to keep poachers, loggers, livestock grazers, and miners from making regular intrusions into the park. In order to protect the park, the military superintendents recommended reducing its boundaries, throwing out any lands that could be developed or were coveted by commercial interests.

In 1905, an act of Congress removed some 542 square miles, including important wildlife winter habitat along the Merced River, plus some of the higher mountain terrain east of Tioga Pass and south of the present park borders by Mount Ritter. Another small reduction took place in 1906 to facilitate logging along the Wawona Road. Altogether, various acts of Congress reduced Yosemite's original boundaries by one-third.

The tension between preservation and greater development has always dogged national parks. It has always been difficult to draw the line between making parks accessible enough for people to enjoy and overdevelopment that threatens the beauty the parks were established to protect.

From hotel owner James Hutchings's battle to gain control of land for development to more recent controversies over excessive development in the valley, the National Park Service has been involved in a love-hate relationship with concessionaires. Concessions provide the services that tourists visiting a park require—food, shelter, equipment, and services. But at the same time such services can create a demand

The Ahwahnee Hotel in the Yosemite Valley is named after a village of the Ahwahneechee Indians, a sub-tribe of the Miwok who resided in the Yosemite Valley.

where none exists. For example, there was not a huge demand for downhill skiing in Yosemite, yet concessionaires, who wanted to increase winter use of the park to extend their business seasons, drove the creation of the Badger Pass ski area.

The Park Service often had a reason to support concessionaires' desire to increase development. When the national parks were first established, the agency and the parks it managed were always under attack by competing industries and agencies for control of the landscape. In order to build a constituency for the parks, the Park Service often sought to draw crowds by any means possible. A zoo in the Yosemite Valley and "Indian Days," where pony races and powwows were staged, were examples of this effort to attract visitors.

Since the turn of the century, there have been some who express dismay over the growing development of the Yosemite Valley. By the 1950s, even the top officials in the Park Service were beginning to question whether development in the valley had gone too far. In 1954, Director Newton Drury called for the removal of government facilities out of the valley, plus the closing of some lodges, tourist shows that featured entertainers, and a dance hall at Camp Curry, in an effort to reduce their impact on the park's natural features.

Despite its general philosophy of reducing development, the Park Service often had a difficult time resisting concessionaire-generated expansion of park use. In 1980, the Park Service released its master plan that called for, among other things, a scaling back of development in the valley and the movement of many facilities to nearby communities outside of the park. Despite the plan, not much really happened, as concessionaires and their allies in Congress brought pressure to bear upon the agency. In 2000, the Park Service was back with another plan that called for scaling down of facilities in the valley. Whether this plan will result in any significant movement of development out of the park remains to be seen.

Right:
Backpackers hike in the Hetch Hetchy Valley near Wapama Falls. The northern section of the park, including Hetch Hetchy Valley, receives far lighter recreational use than the Tuolumne Meadows and Yosemite Valley regions.

Facing page:
The Yosemite Valley was named by members of the 1851 Mariposa Battalion. After debating among themselves what to call the place, they decided to call it Yosemity for the Indian band that lived there.

Wildlife Management in Yosemite

Yosemite was originally set aside to protect grand scenery, including protecting the forests from loggers and the flowery meadows from the ravages of sheep. But there was little thought given to the park's role in protecting wildlife. The value of Yosemite as a biological reserve grew in proportion to the losses of habitat outside of the park.

In 1914, University of California biologist Joseph Grinnell proposed a zoological survey of the park to inventory the wildlife of the region. The first part of the survey was completed by 1916. Grinnell, along with his assistant Tracy Stoner, published an article in *Science Magazine* arguing that one of the prime values of national parks was their scientific importance as a benchmark against which manipulated and developed landscapes could be measured. They argued strenuously for limited manipulation of the landscape and for the protection of all park wildlife—including predators. They fought not only the killing of native animals but the introduction of exotic animals as well.

For instance, Grinnell battled on behalf of the park's black bears. Garbage was used to attract bears into the valley where they could be viewed in "bear shows." Tourists sat in bleachers and watched the bears rummage through the garbage heaps. They also regularly fed black bears. In 1929, more than eighty people were treated for bear injuries received in the park.

Grinnell argued that bear-human conflicts could be significantly reduced by requiring campers to keep food from the animals. Eventually Yosemite's administration followed Grinnell's advice, ending the bear shows in 1940. It later enacted regulations designed to keep bears and human food separate; it enforced measures that prohibited the feeding of animals, required bear-proof garbage cans in campgrounds, and directed back-country campers to hang food supplies out of the animals' reach.

Yosemite Wildlife

The wildlife of Yosemite enlivens the forest and meadows. It is what makes Yosemite more than dead scenery. Diverse elevations create diverse habitat, so it is not surprising that Yosemite supports an array of species, including 85 mammals, 150 birds, 22 reptiles, 11 amphibians, and 6 native species of fish.

When Yosemite was first designated a park, the only native fish were rainbow trout, Sacramento squawfish, hardhead, California roach, Sacramento sucker, and riffle sculpin. Fish stocking introduced trout to many formally barren streams and lakes. Of the 1,591 lakes in the park, 125 contain fish. Rainbow is the most common species with 50 lakes harboring this native fish. Another 49 lakes are home to brook trout, a fish native to the eastern United States and widely stocked in the West. Cutthroat trout are in one lake and golden trout in two. Both fish are native to the Sierra Nevada but not Yosemite. Brown trout are found in some streams and lakes as well.

In some cases, the stocked species have harmed native fish, and it may have harmed frogs and other wildlife. The effects on aquatic invertebrates is unknown, but likely severe. The National Park Service no longer stocks many of the higher-elevation lakes and streams and is allowing populations to die out if they are not self-sustaining.

Terrestrial wildlife is strongly associated with various vegetation zones. Beginning at the low-elevation oak woodlands and chaparral along the Merced River Gorge, one may encounter scrub jays, Nuttall's woodpeckers, acorn woodpeckers, Hutton's vireos, California thrashers, and brown towhees. Mammals include spotted bats, California massif bats, and Yuma myotis, plus ring tails, raccoons, mountain lions, bobcats, dusky-footed woodrats, spotted skunks, and mule deer.

In the pine and oak woodlands of the Yosemite Valley and the South Fork of the Merced Valley near Wawona, you may encounter many of the

With the extirpation of wolves from California, mountain lions are now one of the few remaining large predators. Unlike wolves, which rely primarily upon speed to capture prey on the run, mountain lions stalk their quarry, making a sudden rush to ambush unsuspecting prey. Mountain lions feed primarily on mule deer.

The yellow-bellied marmot is a relative of the familiar eastern ground hog. The marmot lives in colonies among rock slides. A vegetarian that hibernates all winter, it must build up sufficient fat reserves during the short summer season. Marmots that fail to put on enough fat may die of "starvation" in their winter burrows.

The snowshoe hare, sometimes called the snowshoe rabbit, uses its large hind feet to stay afloat on deep snow. The hare is brown in summer but changes to white in winter. It is most common in the red fir and lodgepole forests of the sub-alpine vegetation zone.

same animals as along the Merced Gorge, including mule deer, mountain lions, and Bota's pocket gophers. Also common are bobcats and coyotes.

A species common along streams is the playful and cheery dipper. A member of the wren family, the dipper dives into the stream and walks along the bottom, feeding on aquatic insects.

Perhaps the animal that generates the most interest and excitement is the black bear. Black bears come in a variety of color phases, including black but also cinnamon, brown, and even blonde. They are largely vegetarian, feeding on a variety of foods, from white pine cones to roots and berries. They will on occasion, however, kill deer fawns, ground squirrels, and other animals.

It is normal for the lower mixed conifer zone to experience periodic fires. Fires benefit not only the plant communities but wildlife as well. Bark boring beetles increase after a blaze, which in turn attracts many different

woodpeckers, including black-backed, hairy, downy, and white-headed. The cavities they create in the snags become the nesting habitat for other species, such as tree swallows, mountain chickadees, red-breasted nuthatches, and pygmy owls. Flying squirrels also reside in old woodpecker cavities. Townsend solitaire and western wood pewees swoop in and target the flying insects in the newly open habitat created by the fire. As the vegetation grows back, nesting habitat is created for shrub-loving species like Nashville warblers and mountain quail.

Climbing higher into the mountains, you enter the higher-elevation mixed conifer forests of Jeffrey pine, red fir, and white fir, and the subalpine forests of mountain hemlock and lodgepole pine. Here one can find Pacific fishers, red foxes, Douglas squirrels, northern flying squirrels, snowshoe hares, porcupines, yellow-bellied marmots, and long-tailed weasels. There are three ground squirrels found in Yosemite, and two inhabit the mixed conifer and subalpine zones—the golden-mantled and the Belding's ground squirrels.

Birds seen occasionally among these forested habitats include the goshawk and great gray owl. Other common birds of this zone are the Cassin finch, Townsend's solitaire, Lincoln sparrow, and raven. Mountain chickadees and red-breasted nuthatches also inhabit this zone, probing the bark for insects and eating conifer seeds. At the higher elevations, especially among the white bark pine forests, you may see and more likely hear the raucous Clark's nutcracker.

Up above timberline, you may see another large hare—the white-tailed jackrabbit, a species typical of open grasslands in places like Montana and Wyoming. Like the snowshoe hare, the white-tailed jackrabbit turns white in the winter. Other species common in the subalpine to alpine zone are the water pipit, white-tailed ptarmigan, rosy finch, blue grouse, alpine chipmunk, pika, mountain pocket gopher, and Mount Lyell shrew.

One of the rarest mammals found in the subalpine and alpine zone of Yosemite is the Sierra Nevada red fox. This native fox is an Ice Age relict that is genetically different from the eastern red fox of the lowlands. Elu-

Top left:
A baby Belding's ground squirrel stands alert at its burrow.

Bottom left:
Whitetail ptarmigan are common in mountains from Montana north to Alaska. They are not native to the Sierra Nevada but were introduced into the high country near Saddlebag Lake just east of the park. They are now occasionally seen in alpine regions along the park's eastern border.

Facing page:
Black bears, despite their name, come in various color phases, including cinnamon, brown, blonde, bluish, and even white. The most common color phases found in Yosemite are brown and black. Extremely intelligent and resourceful, black bears will aggressively seek out human food sources, occasionally prying off doors of vehicles to get at food stored inside. They show amazing discrimination, breaking into only those cars that offer potential food. When peering into car windows, they are able to distinguish coolers of food from suitcases and other gear.

sive and seldom seen, the Sierra Nevada fox has several color morphs and is not always red.

Although Yosemite is one of the largest unfragmented blocks of habitat in the Sierra Nevada, park designation came too late to save all the wildlife that once resided here. The bighorn sheep that once roamed the high country succumbed to diseases transmitted by domestic sheep. The last grizzly bear in Yosemite was killed in 1895. Wolves, although never common, also were gone by the turn of the century. The last wolverine recorded for Yosemite was seen in the 1970s. No breeding pairs of the harlequin duck have been observed in Yosemite in decades. Also gone are the Bell's vireo and California condor.

But without dwelling too much on what isn't here, we can rejoice on what is still present.

Boulders on Mount Hoffmann frame Clouds Rest and Half Dome. Mount Hoffmann (10,850 feet) was named for a member of the Whitney Expedition that climbed the peak during an 1863 mapping expedition to the Yosemite region.

Grinnell was also a staunch proponent of public education and outreach. He recommended that the park hire a naturalist, who would "help awaken people to the livelier interest in wild life, and to a healthy and intelligent curiosity about things of nature." Taking a clue from Grinnell, in 1920, Yosemite established its first interpretation program.

Today, Yosemite wildlife is now managed largely along the lines that Grinnell outlined decades ago.

Yosemite Today and Tomorrow

What the various controversies over the years demonstrate is that there is never a time when Yosemite is fully protected and secure. There are few full frontal attacks on the park any longer, but the park's values are still incrementally eroded by what may seem at first to be minor intrusions.

However, in many respects the valley and highlands are in better condition today than when the park was first established. Over the years, changing values have led to changes in the park management's guiding principles, which moved towards greater protection of ecological reserves. Natural processes such as wildfires have been reintroduced. The stocking of exotic fish is no longer tolerated. Feeding bears is discouraged. Cattle no longer graze in the valley. People can't park their cars on meadows and camp anywhere they choose, as once was standard practice.

In 1984, Congress created the Yosemite Wilderness, preventing future development of most of the park's backcountry; some 94 percent of the park is designated wilderness that precludes the use of motorized vehicles and other development. Most development is now focused on the Yosemite Valley, which occupies only one percent of the park's total area.

The park was named a World Heritage Site in 1984, making it part of an international effort to protect representative landscapes around the world for future generations. In addition, in 1984, the main stem of the Tuolumne River and the Dana and Lyell Forks were added to the National Wild and Scenic Rivers system. In 1987, an additional 114 miles of the main stem and the south fork of the Merced were also designated part of this system.

Yosemite has been dazzling visitors since the first people entered the valley, and it continues to be an international icon of beauty and preservation. There is simply no more spectacular combination of rivers, forests, cliffs, waterfalls, granite, and mountains on earth; in Yosemite, all these elements come together to create one of the grandest natural settings in the world. Overall, Yosemite has better protection today than ever before, and for those who seek out the mountains, as John Muir admonished, there is still plenty to discover and enjoy.

Mount Starr King lies along the Illilouette Creek drainage. Thomas Starr King was a well-known preacher from Boston who visited the Yosemite region in 1860. He helped to publicize the Yosemite Valley and its scenic wonders.

Yosemite's Waterfalls

Of all Yosemite's natural features, perhaps the waterfalls and cascades are the most popular with visitors. There is no doubt that Yosemite's falls are numerous and spectacular. Yosemite Falls is certainly one of the ten highest falls in the world; some also consider Sentinel and Ribbon Falls to be among the world's highest. The Yosemite Valley reputedly contains more waterfalls than any other similar-sized area in the world.

Most of the park's falls depend upon snowmelt and reach their maximum volume in May. Some, like Nevada Fall, persist year round because they have large drainages with major streams as their source, but others, including Yosemite and Ribbon Falls, tend to disappear altogether or at best become anemic slender slivers of water in the summer and fall.

The highest and most dramatic falls in the valley originate in hanging valleys carved by glaciers, often thousands of feet above the valley floor. Yosemite and Bridalveil both originate in hanging valleys. The second kind of falls common in the valley are the stair-step falls, like Vernal and Nevada Falls, which were created when glaciers took chunks of rock out of parts of the valley in a stairway fashion.

Ribbon Fall is the highest free-leaping waterfall in the park. It drops 1,612 feet in a free-fall in an alcove by El Capitan.

There are other spectacular falls in the park outside of the Yosemite Valley. Tueeulala Falls drops nearly 1,000 feet on the cliffs of the Hetch Hetchy Valley. Wapama Falls, also flowing into Hetch Hetchy Reservoir, drops an impressive 1,700 feet in a series of cascades.

The Grand Canyon of the Tuolumne River also supports four magnificent falls. The best known is Waterwheel Falls, reachable only by a strenuous 18.6-mile round-trip hike.

The other major fall in the Upper Merced Valley is 370-foot Illilouette Fall. This lovely fall carries the greatest water flow of any Merced River tributary and is particularly spectacular in the spring when flows are highest. The fall is hidden in a side canyon and can be seen from the Panaroma Trail.

Wapama Falls, one of the park's most dramatic and thunderous, drops into the Hetch Hetchy Valley. Due to its location in the little-visited Hetch Hetchy Valley few people actually see it, although it is easily one of the more spectacular falls in the park.

Below the Valley:

Southern Yosemite

Lacking such striking landmarks as El Capitan and Half Dome, Yosemite's southwest corner, where the Wawona historic district and the Mariposa Grove of Giant Sequoias are found, draws fewer people. Most visitors pass through the area while accessing the park on Highway 41. Yet it would be a shame to rush through this part of the park without dallying to explore some its features.

The site most people notice is the Wawona Hotel. The large California Victorian building with its broad porches lies just off Highway 41, some thirty miles south of the Yosemite Valley. The original owner, Galen Clark, was known as "the Guardian of Yosemite" and homesteaded the area in 1856. Clark later discovered the Mariposa Grove and became one of the park's first "rangers." He built the first hotel on the site in 1876, but eventually sold it to new owners, who upgraded the facility. Today the Wawona site features the hotel, now a National Historic Landmark, and Clark's cabin.

Wawona is also the location of the Pioneer Yosemite History Center—buildings from various parts of the park were relocated here to create a living history site. During the summer, interpreters in period costumes present demonstrations that bring Yosemite's colorful history to life. You can also see a covered bridge, originally constructed by Galen Clark, over the South Fork of the Merced River.

Because so much of the land around Wawona was homesteaded, and hence private land, the area was not originally part of the park. Some 8,785 acres were purchased in 1932 and brought under park control.

Just six miles southwest of Wawona is the Mariposa Grove. It protects one of seventy-five sequoia groves found along the west slope of the Sierra Nevada. The Mariposa Grove lies between 5,500 and 7,000 feet in elevation and contains—according to one count—481 mature trees. The Mariposa Grove was discovered by Clark while on a hunting trip in 1857. Soon the grove was a must-see for all visitors coming to Yosemite. The grove was included in the original legislation in 1864 that protected Yosemite Valley as a California state park, and it was one of the special features that helped garner national park protection for the entire Yosemite area.

Even without sequoia, the forests of Yosemite are notable. The Sierran forest is one of the most diverse and magnificent in the United States. Giant sugar pine (most outside of the park have been logged away) compete for attention with ponderosa pine, Jeffrey pine, incense cedar, red fir, and white pine. Depending on the micro-habitat, mixed in among these forest giants are beautiful hardwoods, including canyon oak, black oak, Pacific dogwood, bigtooth maple, and others.

One of the best ways to experience these forests is to hike some of the lower-elevation trails in the southern part of the park. The Moraine Meadows trail to Chilnualna Fall begins near Wawona and is a moderate day hike through some pretty Sierra Nevada forests to one of the highest falls outside of the Yosemite Valley. Looking up through sunlit needles of pine or seeing the reddish orange of ponderosa pine bark against a blue sky will make for an unforgettable day. The hike leaves the cascading Chilnualna Creek for a few miles before swinging back to the falls, so make sure you have plenty of water. The trail continues beyond the falls to the southern edge of the Yosemite high country near Fernandez Pass, passing a series of lakes and intersecting with numerous other trails that head into the Ansel Adams Wilderness and Devil's Post Pile area.

The Alder Creek trail connects Wawona with the Yosemite Valley via Bridalveil Creek. It follows an old railroad grade that once facilitated extensive logging within the park. This dark period in park history began during World War I and continued into the 1920s. Logging was justified in the name of the war effort, and giant sugar pine were cut from the park's forests. The logging continued until 1930 when John D. Rockefeller Jr. stepped in to buy out the logging companies' timber rights.

The Alder Creek trail passes through drier and more open forests than the Chilnualna Fall trail and is a good springtime hike. Ponderosa pine along with incense cedar and black oak prevail along this trail.

Previous page:

A timberline snag lies on Horse Ridge. Horse Ridge is west of Wawona and reachable by trail from the Glacier Point Road.

The Anderson Building (above) and Artist Building (below) are just two of the old cabins and other buildings moved to their current site near Wawona from other parts of the park to form the Pioneer Yosemite History Center. During the summer months, park interpreters in period costumes provide a living history experience.

Top left:
The Mariposa Grove museum nestles among the towering giant trees.

Bottom left:
Sequoias are arguably the largest living things in the world. Since they may live three thousand years and continue to add girth until death, they can and do attain huge proportions. Young sequoias grow two feet a year, and by the time they are fifty years old, they may tower more than one hundred feet. The tree reaches its maximum height at about eight hundred years of age, at which point its height may exceed three hundred feet. In some cases, individual branches on these immense trees are larger than entire trees elsewhere.

Facing page:
The Mariposa Grove is by far the largest of Yosemite's three sequoia groves.

Above:
Sugar pine, another fire-adapted species, is a common associate of the sequoias. Sugar pines sport narrow cones that are up to two feet long. Due to their large size, one doesn't want to wander among a sugar pine forest during a windstorm.

Facing page:
A skier in the Mariposa Grove is dwarfed by the immensity of the giant sequoias. Sequoias tend to be found in an elevation belt where snowfall is greatest and soils are deep, perhaps reflecting their need for saturated soils to help them get through the dry Sierran summer.

Above:
The Grizzly Giant bears scars of a fire. As a species adapted to fire, the sequoia has few peers. The trees are armored with thick bark—often up to two feet thick—that insulates the tree's inner living tissue from all but the hottest blazes. The trees also self-prune; older trees lose their lower limbs, removing a potential "ladder" that would allow flames to reach the fire-sensitive crown.

Western white pine on Buena Vista Ridge frames the Clark Range. The Clark Range is named for Galen Clark. While in his forties, Clark suffered from a lung ailment and was told he would die within a few months. Wanting to spend his last days in the beauty of the mountains, he built a cabin near present-day Wawona. He was later appointed the first "guardian" of Yosemite by the State of California.

A backpacker, exploring off trail some of the park's backcountry near Hart Lake, contemplates her route. Off-trail travel in the higher parts of Yosemite is relatively easy because of the abundance of bare rock and open, brush-free forests.

The Incomparable Yosemite Valley

There are other beautiful valleys in the Sierra Nevada, but none have the same proportions, dimensions, and spectacular setting as the Yosemite Valley. Called the "incomparable valley" by John Muir, it is the most-visited area of Yosemite National Park and an American icon.

The Yosemite Valley is about seven miles long and is in most areas a mile or less wide. It lies at about 4,000 feet in elevation. Though its 700 or so acres compose only 1 percent of the 700,000-plus-acre park, the valley's value and recognition goes well beyond its small area.

Entering Yosemite National Park by way of Highway 41 from Fresno and Wawona offers an unbelievable first glimpse at what is arguably the most magnificent panorama in the entire West. Immediately after the Wawona Tunnel is a large parking area; from this vantage point, framed by tall pines, the entire Yosemite Valley is spread before you. Off to the right is Bridalveil Fall, with El Capitan's sheer cliffs opposite it on the north side of the valley. Far down the valley, Half Dome rises above other domes and peaks.

The grand story of the valley's geological formation can be seen from this one observation point. Downstream from the Wawona Tunnel, the Merced River cuts through a steep, V-shaped canyon, while upstream, the valley is wide and U-shaped—a classic signature of glaciation.

The glacier that polished and scarped the Yosemite Valley retreated 14,000 years ago. It remained stationary for a while between Bridalveil and El Capitan meadows, leaving behind loose debris deposits called recessional moraine. Moraines created a natural dam on the Merced River between Bridalveil Fall and El Capitan. The resulting lake gradually filled with sediments, creating the nearly level valley floor we find today. Even as recently as 100 years ago, the valley floor was considerably wetter than at present, but the moraine was dynamited to hasten the drainage of the river and dry up the swampy areas. This drainage has contributed to a rapid down-cutting of the river channel, which has led to many changes in the river hydrology both up- and downstream from this site.

Because the lower valley was originally so swampy, most of the existing development in the valley lies in its upper third. Here you find facilities such as the Park Service's visitor center, a museum, campgrounds, stores, restaurants, and hotels such as the Ahwahnee Hotel. This complex is something analogous to a small city, especially in summer when nearly every campsite and hotel room is full. A free shuttle bus provides access to all trailheads, campgrounds, the visitor center, and other stations. A bike path circles the valley, providing a peaceful way to enjoy Yosemite's splendors.

A number of different hikes emanate from the Park Service complex. The most popular is the hike up the Mist Trail to Vernal and Nevada Falls. Most people only hike the 0.7 of a mile to a bridge across the Merced River that affords a spectacular view of Vernal Fall. However, if you have more time and energy, it is definitely worth going the extra mile and a half to Nevada Fall.

The quarter-mile hike to the base of Yosemite Falls perhaps offers the greatest rewards for the effort of any hike in the park. The trail leads to the foot of Lower Yosemite Fall, where the crescendo of crashing waves pound the cliff face with an overwhelming sound and fury.

Another popular but more peaceful hike is the half-mile stroll on a paved trail from Happy Isles to Mirror Lake, which offers fantastic views of Half Dome. The trail has its own rewards as it traverses lovely forests of oaks, sugar pine, ponderosa pine, and incense cedar.

A more demanding hike is the Yosemite Falls Trail, which begins near Sunnyside Campground and switchbacks up the sheer north face of the Yosemite Valley. This trail is not for the faint of heart, as it contours the cliff face with sharp drop-offs, but the views all along the route are terrific. The 3.6-mile trail climbs 2,700 feet and takes hikers to the very brink of Yosemite Falls.

Spend a day or spend a month—either way, few would argue with John Muir's assessment that Yosemite is the "incomparable valley."

Previous page:

The Yosemite Valley is a classic glacier-carved valley. Glaciers often filled an entire valley wall to wall, plucking and gouging the sides and bottom as they moved. The remaining broad, steep-walled valleys are characteristically U-shaped.

A black oak displays autumn leaves along the Merced River. Oak acorns were an important food resource for native people living in the valley as well as many wildlife species, including bear, deer, and squirrel.

Above:

After many years of tumbling over boulders, the river has worn smooth the rough edges of the rock.

Facing page:

The Merced River rushes over boulders in the lower valley. The gradient of the stream in the lower valley was increased substantially when a moraine blocked the river near El Capitan, creating a swampy area. Early residents of the valley blasted away the moraine to drain the swamp.

Above:
A cascade is formed on the Merced River near El Portal, by the park's western entrance.

Right:
Bracken fern grows along the Merced River. Bracken fern frequently invades recently burned areas, growing in dense clusters. In spring the uncurling leaves known as "fiddleheads" are sometimes collected and eaten. Some native people also collected and roasted the roots.

Facing page:
Fallen maple leaves adorn a mossy boulder on the riverbank.

Top right:

The Merced roars during its annual spring flood. These floods are the result of snow-melt in the high country and typically peak in May or June. The other type of flood is known as a rain-on-snow event. These floods can occur anytime from September to April. They are the result of heavy, warm rain falling on snow, causing rapid snowmelt, which then combines with the rain run-off to form a high-water flow.

Bottom right:

Merced floodwaters race past a leafless dogwood. Floodwaters naturally rejuvenate plant communities by adding new nutrients and soaking soils. They move and create woody debris that is important habitat for wildlife and fish.

Bigleaf maple is a common species in the forests of western Oregon and western Washington, but restricted in the Sierra Nevada to moist, riparian areas at low to middle elevations.

Lupine grow profusely from a burn near Big Meadow. Fire opens up the forest, reduces competition among some plants, and helps to recycle nutrients. In fact, rather than being a "disaster," fire helps to rejuvenate Yosemite's ecosystems.

Top left:
With few cracks, El Capitan's granite face thwarts erosion and makes it one of the sheerest on earth. The lack of cracks and ledges frustrated climbers for decades, and the face was only scaled for the first time in 1958.

Bottom left:
The quiet waters of the Merced provide a mirror for the face of El Capitan.

Facing page:
After Half Dome, El Capitan is one of the most famous features in the Yosemite Valley. According to one interpretation, "El Capitan" is a translation of the Indian name for the mountain they called "Rock Chief" for its presumed human-like profile.

The Yosemite Valley, as seen from Inspiration Point, is flanked by El Capitan and Bridalveil Fall. It was near this same point that the members of the Mariposa Battalion first beheld the valley in 1851.

Bridalveil Fall tumbles 620 feet into the Yosemite Valley. The falls drop from a glacially created side valley known as a hanging valley. Many tributary glaciers contributed to the main glacier that once filled the Yosemite Valley. Because these tributary glaciers were smaller than the main one, they excavated proportionally shallower valleys alongside and above the main valley. After all the glaciers melted away, the valleys once holding tributary glaciers were left high and dry, "hanging" hundreds of feet above the valley floor.

Black oak in the Yosemite Valley frames the Cathedral Spires, named by James Hutchings in 1862. Hutchings, who was one of the valley's early boosters, operated a hotel in the valley and published a tourism promotion magazine on California.

Cattails carpet the Yosemite Valley in front of Sentinel Rock, named for its presumed likeness to a watchtower.

In the absence of fire, trees such as ponderosa pine begin to invade the meadows of the Yosemite Valley. Prior to fire suppression, fires ignited by both human and natural causes burned through lower elevation terrain like the Yosemite Valley every ten to twenty years, if not more frequently. These fires helped maintain the natural meadows and open forest groves that are some of the pleasing characteristics of the Yosemite landscapes. Today the Park Service periodically sets prescribed burns designed to mimic the natural fire regime.

Above left:

The ponderosa pine has three- to six-inch cones.

Top left and right:

Ponderosa pine have deep taproots that ensure survival during the summer drought. A three-inch sapling may have roots more than two feet long.

The tree is adapted to periodic fire. The lower boles are typically free of branches to prevent ground blazes from leaping up into the crowns. The thick, flaky bark acts as insulation. As the bark heats up, the outer layers flip off just before they would ignite. By these means, the tree can tolerate low-intensity blazes that are fairly regular occurrences over much of its natural range.

Above and facing page:
Yosemite Falls is the most famous of the valley's waterfalls. It drops 2,425 feet in three separate leaps from the rim of the valley to the floor below. It is not only the highest falls in the park, it is the highest in North America and one of the ten highest in the entire world.

Above:

The steep, 3.6-mile Yosemite Falls Trail has many switchbacks and gains 2,700 feet as it climbs up the face of the north wall of the valley, eventually leading to the brink of the Upper Yosemite Fall.

Facing page:

Yosemite Falls hides in a dark recess during a winter sunset.

Above:
The rushing waters of the Merced River below Vernal Fall can be seen along the Mist Trail.

Facing page:
The Merced River tumbles over 317-foot Vernal Fall, which reaches its peak volume in the spring. Like many other Yosemite landmarks, the fall was named by Mariposa Battalion member Lafayette Bunnell, who thought its cool mist contrasted with the heat of the mid-day sun.

Above:

Hikers view Liberty Cap from along the John Muir Trail.

Facing page:

Liberty Cap is an example of a roche moutonnées. Looking something like grazing sheep, roche moutonnées are created when glaciers smooth the tops of rocky ridges into gently rising ridges, while the descending slope is made steeped and rough.

Liberty Cap, Nevada Fall, and the Yosemite high country can be seen in a single view through the sugar pine boughs near Glacier Point.

Above:
From Glacier Point, crowds gather to watch the sun set on Half Dome, as a park ranger offers details about the famous formation.

Facing page:
Yosemite's most famous rock consists of Half Dome Granodiorite, a kind of granitic rock. It is 87 million years old—much younger than other rock exposures in the valley. This type of rock is found throughout the upper end of the Yosemite Valley.

Above:
Half Dome rises to 8,842 feet, more than 4,770 feet above Tenaya Canyon. The rounded side of the dome can be seen from Olmsted Point.

Clouds Rest and Half Dome are seen in this view from Olmsted Point. The foreground shows the distinctive jointing, or cracking, in the granite that has produced many of the park's features. Joints are fractures in the bedrock, and these zones of shattered rock offer points of weakness that invite erosion. Both the sheer face of Half Dome and the cliffs of El Capitan were created by erosion along major joint systems.

Mountain hemlock grows along the Mount Hoffmann Trail. More typical of the Pacific Northwest and Alaska coastal forests, mountain hemlock is rare in the Sierra Nevada and reaches its most southern limits in the vicinity of Yosemite National Park. The presence of mountain hemlock in Yosemite National Park is partially a result of geology: The gap in the Coast Range created by San Francisco Bay permits moist winter storms to pass unimpeded through the Central Valley and drop huge amounts of snow upon the slopes of the central Sierra Nevada, including the Yosemite region. The deeper snow pack creates conditions conducive to the growth of mountain hemlock.

Above:
Seen close up, the lichen Letheria vulpinus on incense cedar bark makes for a beautiful abstraction.

Right:
Incense cedar is a major component of mixed conifer forest, such as the vegetation zone along Tenaya Creek. Incense cedar boles are cinnamon red and deeply furrowed. Its leaves are lacy looking with flattened scales. It can germinate in both sun and shade, making it one of the most abundant species in the Yosemite region.

Above:
Ferns crowd the base of an incense cedar.

Above:
Autumn maple leaves cover a boulder along Tenaya Creek, creating an unusual pattern.

Left:
The jumble of unsorted boulders seen along Tenaya Creek is an example of moraine, deposits left by retreating glaciers.

The High Country:

Tuolumne Meadows and Beyond

Most of Yosemite beyond the valley lies at 8,000 feet or higher in elevation. The highest peaks tower to cloud-scraping heights of 13,000 feet or more.

There is a good reason why so much of Yosemite consists of high country. When the park was created, the usual criteria for including any land in preservation scheme were, "Is it essentially worthless for other resource extraction?" and "Is it scenic?" Since most of the lower-elevation lands in the Sierra Nevada along the Merced and Tuolumne Rivers were considered valuable for gold and timber production, they were excluded from the park. On the other hand, the high, rocky alpine country lacked minerals, had little in the way of timber value, and was only marginal for sheep grazing due to the short snow-free summer season. In general, the low commodity value of most of Yosemite's high-country landscape permitted it to be included in the park. When it came to the second criteria—scenery—there was no dispute. Yosemite's high country was magnificent.

The lands that make up Yosemite were scoured by Ice Age glaciers, and small glaciers still reside in the highest north-facing basins. One of the residual effects of this glaciation was that the top soil was scraped away to expose bare rock. The sparsely vegetated high country is a showcase of this glacier-carved rock, with pockets of timber interspersed by slabs of granite, mountain meadows, and numerous ponds and lakes.

In the little forest that exists above 8,000 feet in elevation is mountain hemlock and whitebark pine. But if you were to guess that the tree before you was a lodgepole pine, you would probably be correct nine times out of ten. Lodgepole pine forests are known for their general lack of other vegetation. Some biologists consider them "biological deserts." Among these trees almost nothing grows on the forest floor.

Beyond the lodgepole pine cover, you will find numerous meadows full of wildflowers. False hellebore and bluebells dominate the deeper soils. Many of the grassy meadows are actually composed of sedges, as well as many different ground-hugging flowers.

The centerpiece of the high country and the part that most visitors see is Tuolumne Meadows and the Tioga Pass area that is bisected by Highway 126 or the Tioga Pass Road. A visitor center, campground, food store, and lodge are all located in this area.

Given its central location, a host of trails radiate from the Tuolumne Meadows area. A number of short trails offer outstanding views. Some say the panorama from Lembert Dome is the finest view in the park that can be accessed for so little effort. More demanding, but no less spectacular is the hike up 13,053-foot Mount Dana, the second-highest peak in the park. The 360-degree view from the summit provides a sweeping spectacle of the entire Sierra Nevada, stretching south towards Mount Maclure and Mount Lyell and north towards Matterhorn Peak.

Not all trails ascend peaks. Some just stay along the valley bottoms. The most famous of these pathways is the John Muir Trail, which begins outside the park on Mount Whitney and travels more than 200 miles through the high country of the Sierra Nevada to end in the Yosemite Valley. This "pathway to the sky" takes hikers to points from which they can climb 13,114-foot Mount Lyell, the highest peak in the park. Lyell lies at the apex of the Yosemite back country, where the Clark Range and the Cathedral Range collide.

The really high country lies both north and south of Tuolumne Meadows. For those looking for the ultimate solitude, the canyons and valleys north and east of the Tuolumne River are among the most remote and least traveled parts of the park. In particular the Upper Matterhorn Canyon offers some of the greatest grandeur and seclusion found any place in the park. Some of the lakes in this area can be reached only by cross-country hiking, which is relatively easy given the open nature of the forests and great amount of bare rock.

Whether they just drive through Tuolumne Meadows or spend weeks exploring the high country, most visitors agree that these subalpine and alpine areas of the park rival the Yosemite Valley for scenic splendor.

Previous page:

The grandeur of Tuolumne Meadows spreads out behind granite boulders near Tioga Pass.

Facing page:

Looking north from Mount Hoffmann, one can see across the glaciated basins and peaks of the Yosemite high country.

Above and facing page:
Pine seedlings grow from joints in the granite above Tenaya Lake. As they grow, their roots help to pry apart the rock, exposing the rock to greater erosion. Over time rocks are crumbled into soil.

Above:
A pine clings to the slope of a nameless peak above Tenaya Lake.

Above:

Rock carried frozen in the bottom and sides of a glacier works like a giant rasp, smoothing and polishing the underlying bedrock. Glacier "tracks"—parallel lines and scratches on the rock—are readily apparent throughout Yosemite. In other places "chatter marks"—deeper, unidirectional, sequential gouges carved into the rock—mark the passage of the glacier.

Left:

Polly Dome and Pywiak Dome rise above the entrance to Tuolumne Meadows. Domes are created by the unloading of overlying rock; the relieving pressure causes the granite to be shed in layers along joints in the bedrock.

Above and facing page:

Glacial erratics, or out-of-place boulders dropped by glaciers on bedrock, are abundant in Yosemite. These were dropped on the granite shores of Tenaya Lake and on a bare slope nearby.

Above:

A boulder frames the higher reaches of the Cathedral Range.

Facing page:

A peak in the Cathedral Range rises behind Fletcher Creek.

Above:

A hiker travels on the trail above Vogelsang Lake. Vogelsang is an excellent example of a cirque, a lake created when a glacier scooped out the basin the lake now occupies. Where the head of the glacier attaches to the mountainside, water freezes into cracks and joints, prying away rock, which the moving glacier carries downhill imbedded in the ice. By this process the glacier slowly excavates the basin.

Facing page:

Granite boulders can be found along Rafferty Creek on the trail to Vogelsang Lake.

Nelson Lake, seen here at sunset, is reachable only by cross-country travel.

Tuolumne Meadows, at the headwaters of the Tuolumne River, lies at 8,600 feet in elevation and is considered the largest subalpine meadow in the entire Sierra Nevada mountain range. Actually a series of openings, separated by small bands of forest, the meadows stretch for up to twelve miles if the upper portions on the Dana and Lyell Forks are included. Most of these meadows are dominated by grasslike sedges, plus a changing roll call of flowers that brings color throughout the summer.

Top left:

The meadow area was once covered by the sixty-mile-long Tuolumne Glacier. Once the glacier retreated, a series of small lakes was left behind. These lakes later filled to create the smooth surface of the meadow.

Bottom left:

Lodgepole pine is the dominant forest type surrounding Tuolumne Meadows. Most of the meadows occupy sites that are too wet for trees or where cold-air drainage and the subsequent killing frosts limit conifer invasion. No one can say definitively why lodgepole pine are invading this particular spot; many factors may be at work, from the suppression of natural fires to the increased temperatures and drier soil created by global warming.

Above and right:
A passing thunderstorm has covered the ground with hail in Tuolumne Meadows. With their lightning, thunderstorms are the major source of wildfires in Sierra Nevada forests. However, as the case here, such storms are often accompanied by significant hail or rain that quells any fires before they can get started.

Facing page:
Mist obscures Lembert Dome near the head of Tuolumne Meadows.

Top right:

Writing about Tuolumne Meadows, John Muir called it "the most spacious and delightful high pleasure-ground I have yet seen. The air is keen and bracing, yet warm during the day; and though lying high in the sky, the surrounding mountains are so much higher, one feels protected as if in a grand hall."

Bottom right:

The meadows lay along the Mono Trail, an ancient, well-worn travel corridor that Native Americans used to cross the mountains to the basins east of the Sierra Nevada. Sometimes people from both east and west of the mountains met in the meadows to trade. Some groups camped in the meadows for least part of the summer to avoid the heat of lower elevations and to hunt the bighorn sheep that once were thick in the nearby mountains. Evidence of Indian occupation includes obsidian flakes left from the fashioning of arrowheads and mortar holes where people ground up acorns.

Facing page:

Western juniper clings to a rocky slope near Tioga Pass. Juniper berries are a favorite food for birds and other wildlife; ranchers in the Old West often used the tree's rot-resistant wood for fence posts.

Top right:

Exfoliation is a major influence upon Yosemite's features. Exfoliation results when granitic rock, formed under great pressure deep in the earth, is gradually uplifted. As the overlying rock is removed by erosion, pressure is relieved so that the rock peels away along joint-controlled fractures. This progressive peeling away of rock leads to rounded surface or dome, as seen on Lembert Dome.

Bottom right:

The hike to the summit of Lembert Dome is one of the easiest in the park and provides an incredible vista.

Facing page:

Looking northeast from Lembert Dome, the headwaters of Delaney Creek are visible. The creek is named for Pat Delaney, a sheep rancher who employed John Muir as his shepherd in 1869. The job gave Muir his first opportunity to visit the Tuolumne Meadows region.

On the shaded north walls of
Mount Lyell and Mount
Maclure lie some of the largest
glaciers in Yosemite.

Though the last major Ice Age ended thousands of years ago, a slight cooling between 1600 and 1850 led to what is sometimes called the Little Ice Age. During this period of time, small glaciers formed in the Sierra Nevada, including these glaciers on Mount Gibbs and Kuna Peak. These relict glaciers are largely confined to shady north-facing slopes at 11,000 feet or higher.

The view from the shoulder of Mount Dana looks over metavolcanic rocks. Despite Yosemite's fame as one exposed mass of granitic rock, the eastern edge of the park consists of metavolcanic rocks, which contain pockets of gold and other minerals. The area shown in this photo was once scoured by miners looking for outcrops of mineralized rock. This geology affected the history of the park—the original borders of Yosemite were shrunk by as much as a third to accommodate the mining industry.

Above:
A lake nestled below the Kuna Crest sparkles in the sun.

Facing page:
Mono Pass was once the major route across the mountains for Indians and, later, miners. Remains of old mining cabins can still be seen near the pass.

Above top and bottom:
Dana Meadows, pictured here with Mount Dana behind, is really just
an extension of Tuolumne Meadows.

Mount Dana is framed by a timberline snag resting above Gaylor Lake near the park's eastern border. At 13,053 feet, Mount Dana is the second-highest summit in Yosemite National Park. Though steep, the climb to the top of Mount Dana is nothing more than a strenuous hike.

Above:
Sky pilot grows on the summit of Mount Dana. Like other alpine flowers, this plant must endure intense solar radiation that creates hot, dry conditions in the day, with freezing temperatures common at night.

Facing page:
Mammoth Peak, part of the Kuna Crest, provides a majestic backdrop for a wildflower meadow on the slope of Mount Dana.

Above:
Mammoth Peak looms above the Dana Fork.

Right:
The sunrise lights up Mammoth Peak, and both are reflected in the smooth surface of a tarn by Tioga Pass. The tarn was created when glacial ice trapped by a moraine melted.

Above:

Near the timberline at Granite Lakes, a twisted pine highlights the view of a cirque—a bowl-like basin formerly occupied by a glacier.

Facing page:

Gaylor Lake was named for a Yosemite Park ranger who died of a heart attack in 1921 while out on patrol in the park.

Above:

A stone has become wedged in the gnarled surface of a timberline whitebark pine by Tioga Pass.

Facing page:

Fire creates snags that become the home for many wildlife species. More than 25 percent of the birds in the region depend upon cavities in snags for their nest sites. Other animals from flying squirrels to bats may also use fire-created cavities or old snags for homes. When snags fall into streams, they create habitat for many invertebrate species from insects to fish. They also help to slow water and stabilize banks, reducing erosion.

Above:

A granite outcrop by North Peak, along the eastern border of the park, looks as rough and stark as the surface of the moon.

Facing page:

Upper McCabe Lake sits in a granitic basin along the park's eastern border.

The peaks of Shepherd Crest can be seen in a sweeping view from the edge of Virginia Canyon, just west of Summit Lake and Virginia Pass. The range was named for the sheepherders that used to roam below it.

Near the headwaters of Return Creek in Virginia Canyon, metamorphic rocks (dark rocks) lie on top of granitics (white rock). At one time the metamorphic rocks covered all of the granitics now exposed in Yosemite, but subsequent uplift accelerated erosion, which stripped away the metamorphic rock from most parts of the Sierra Nevada.

Bibliography

Ano, Stephen. *Discovering Sierra Trees*. Yosemite National Park: Yosemite Association, 1973.

Bakker, Elna S. *An Island Called California*. Berkeley: University of California Press, 1972.

Barbour, Michael, Bruce Pavik, Frank Drysdale and Susan Lindstrom. *California's Changing Landscapes: Diversity and Conservation of California's Vegetation*. Sacramento: California Native Plant Society, 1993.

Beedy, Edward and Stephen Granholm. *Discovering Sierra Birds*. Yosemite National Park: Yosemite Association, 1985.

Brewer, William H. *Up and Down California in 1860–1864*. Berkeley: University of California Press, 1966.

Chase, J. Smeaton. *Yosemite Trails: Exploring the High Sierra*. Palo Alto, Calif.: Tioga Publishing, 1911.

Farquhar, Francis P. *History of the Sierra Nevada*. Berkeley: University of California Press, 1965.

Fox, Stephen. *The American Conservation Movement: John Muir and His Legacy*. Madison: University of Wisconsin Press, 1981.

Hill, Mary. *Geology of the Sierra Nevada*. Berkeley: University of California Press, 1975.

Huber, N. King. *The Geologic Story of Yosemite*. Yosemite National Park: Yosemite Association, 1989.

Johnston, Verna R. *California Forests and Woodlands: A Natural History*. Berkeley: University of California Press, 1994.

Johnston, Verna R. *Sierra Nevada*. Boston: Houghton-Mifflin Co., 1970.

LeConte, Joseph. *A Journal of Ramblings through the High Sierras of California*. High Sierra Classics Series. Yosemite National Park: Yosemite Association, 1994.

Matthes, Francois E. *The Incomparable Valley: A Geologic Interpretation of the Yosemite*. Berkeley: University of California Press, 1950.

Medley, Steven. *The Complete Guidebook to Yosemite National Park*. Yosemite National Park: Yosemite Association, 1991.

Moore, James G. *Exploring the Highest Sierra*. Stanford, Calif.: Stanford University Press, 2000.

Morgenson, Dana. *Yosemite Wildflower Trails*. Yosemite National Park: Yosemite Association, 1975.

Muir, John. *The Proposed Yosemite National Park: Treasures and Features*. Golden, Colo.: Outbooks, 1986.

Muir, John. *John Muir: The Eight Wilderness Discovery Books*. Seattle: The Mountaineers, 1992.

National Park Service. *Draft Environmental Impact Statement and Comprehensive Management Plan for the Merced Wild and Scenic River*. Yosemite National Park: U.S. Department of the Interior, 2000.

National Park Service. *Draft Yosemite Valley Plan: Supplemental Environmental Impact Statement: Executive Summary*. Yosemite National Park: U.S. Department of the Interior, 2000.

National Park Service. *Yosemite Handbook 138*. Yosemite National Park: U.S. Department of the Interior, 1990.

O'Neill, Elizabeth Stone. *Meadow in the Sky: A History of Yosemite's Tuolumne Meadows Region*. Groveland, Calif.: Albicaulis Press, 1984.

Palmer, Tim. *The Sierra Nevada: A Mountain Journey*. Covelo, Calif.: Island Press, 1988.

Runte, Alfred. *Yosemite: The Embattled Wilderness*. Lincoln: University of Nebraska Press, 1990.

Russell, Carl Parcher. *One Hundred Years in Yosemite: The Story of the Great Park and Its Friends*. High Sierra Classics Series. Yosemite National Park: Yosemite Association, 1992.

Sanborn, Margaret. *Yosemite: Its Discovery, Its Wonders, and Its People*. Yosemite National Park: Yosemite Association, 1989.

Schaffer, Jeffrey P. *Yosemite National Park: A Natural History Guide to Yosemite and Its Trails*. Berkeley, Calif.: Wilderness Press, 1978.

Schaffer, Jeffrey P. *The Geomorphic Evolution of the Yosemite Valley and Sierra Nevada Landscapes: Solving the Riddles in the Rocks*. Berkeley, Calif.: Wilderness Press, 1997.

Schoenherr, Allan A. *A Natural History of California*. Berkeley: University of California Press, 1992.

Storer, Tracy and Robert Usinger. *Sierra Nevada Natural History*. Berkeley: University of California Press, 1964.

Thelander, Carl G. (Ed.) *Life on the Edge: A Guide to California's Endangered Natural Resources*. Santa Cruz, Calif.: Biosystems Books, 1994.

Whitney, Stephen. *The Sierra Nevada: A Naturalist's Guide*. San Francisco: Sierra Club Books 1988.

Wildlands Resources Center. *Status of the Sierra Nevada: Sierra Nevada Ecosystem Project. Final Report to Congress*. Davis, Calif.: University of California, Davis, 1996.

Wuerthner, George. *California's Sierra Nevada*. Helena, Mont.: American & World Geographic Publishing, 1993.

Wuerthner, George. *Yosemite: A Visitor's Companion*. Mechanicsburg, Penn.: Stackpole Books, 1994.

Wuerthner, George. *California Wilderness Areas, Vol. One, Mountains and Coast*. Englewood, Colo.: Westcliffe Publishers, 1997.

Index

Ahwahnee Hotel, 27, 54
bears, black, 28, 31, 33
Big Meadow, 61
bigleaf maple, 61
black oak, 42, 55, 68
Bridalveil Fall, 39, 54, 65, 67
Buena Vista Ridge, 48
Bunnell, Lafayette, 17, 19, 79
Cathedral Range, 96, 105
Cathedral Spires, 68
Chilnualna Fall, 42
cirque, 106, 131
Clark Range, 48, 96
Clark, Galen, 42, 48
Clouds Rest, 34, 87
Dana Fork, 116
Dana Meadows, 124
Delaney Creek, 34, 110, 128
El Capitan, 10, 39, 42, 54, 57, 63, 65, 87
erratics, 10, 103
exfoliation, 116
fern, bracken, 58
fire, 31–32, 47, 61, 72, 73, 112, 133
Fletcher Creek, 105
floods, 60
Gaylor Lake, 125, 131
Glacier Point, 83, 85
glaciers, 22–23, 39, 54, 67, 81, 93, 96, 101, 103, 106, 111, 119, 120
granite, 34, 98, 101, 106, 135
Granite Lakes, 131
granitics, 121, 135, 138
Half Dome, 10, 17, 19, 34, 42, 54, 63, 85, 87
hanging valley, 39, 67
Hetch Hetchy, 24, 26
Horse Ridge, 42
Hutchings, James Mason, 19, 20–21, 22, 26, 68
Illilouette Creek, 37
Illilouette Fall, 39

incense cedar, 42, 54, 90
John Muir Trail, 21, 23, 81, 96
joints, 87, 98, 101, 106
Kuna Crest, 123, 126
Lembert Dome, 96, 112, 116
Liberty Cap, 81, 83
lodgepole pine, 32, 96, 111
Lyell Fork, 34, 110
Mammoth Peak, 126, 128
Mariposa Battalion, 17, 19, 28, 65, 79
Mariposa Grove of Giant Sequoias, 16, 24, 42, 45, 47
Matterhorn Peak, 96
Merced River, 10, 13, 15, 17, 19, 23, 26, 39, 42, 54, 57, 58, 60, 63, 79
metamorphic rocks, 138
metavolcanic rock, 121
Mist Trail, 54, 79
Miwok, 14, 27
Mono Pass, 123
Mono Trail, 114
moraine, 54, 57, 93, 128
Mount Dana, 96, 121, 124, 125, 126
Mount Gibbs, 120
Mount Hoffmann, 19, 34, 96
Mount Lyell, 13, 96, 119
Mount Maclure, 96, 119
Mount Starr King, 19, 37
mountain hemlock, 32, 88, 96
Muir, John, 1, 21–23, 24, 26, 34, 54, 114, 116
National Park Service, 26–27, 30, 72
Nelson Lake, 108
Nevada Fall, 17, 39, 54, 83
North Peak, 135
Olmsted Point, 85, 87
Pacific dogwood, 42
Pioneer Yosemite History Center, 42, 43

Polly Dome, 101
ponderosa pine, 42, 54, 72, 73
Pywiak Dome, 101
Rafferty Creek, 106
Ribbon Fall, 39
roche moutoénees, 81
Sentinel Fall, 39
Sentinel Rock, 71
sequoias, 15–16, 20, 42, 45, 47
Shepherd Crest, 136
snags, 32, 42, 125, 133
sugar pine, 26, 42, 47, 54
tarn, 128
Tenaya Creek, 19, 90, 93
Tenaya Lake, 19, 98, 103
Teneiya, 19
Tioga Pass, 10, 13, 26, 96, 114, 128, 133
Tueeulala Falls, 39
Tuolumne Meadows, 10, 28, 96, 101, 110, 111, 112, 114, 116, 124
Tuolumne River, 13, 17, 23, 24, 34, 39, 96, 110
Upper McCabe Lake, 135
Vernal Fall, 13, 17, 39, 54, 79
Virginia Canyon, 136
Virginia Pass, 136
Vogelsang Lake, 106
Wapama Falls, 28, 39
waterfalls, 34, 39
    see also names of individual waterfalls
Waterwheel Falls, 39
Wawona, 17, 42, 43, 48, 54
Western juniper, 114
Western white pine, 48
Yosemite Falls, 10, 39, 54, 74, 77
    Upper Yosemite Fall, 77
    Lower Yosemite Fall, 54
Yosemite Falls Trail, 54, 77

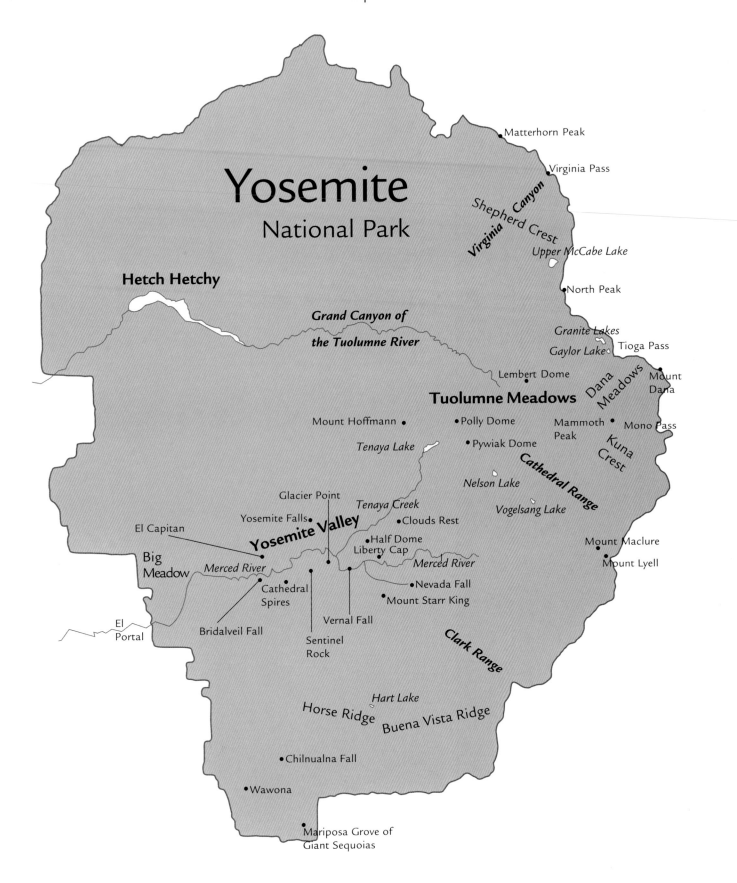

Yosemite
National Park

Matterhorn Peak

Virginia Pass

Shepherd Crest

Virginia Canyon

Upper McCabe Lake

Hetch Hetchy

North Peak

Grand Canyon of
the Tuolumne River

Granite Lakes

Tioga Pass

Gaylor Lake

Lembert Dome

Dana Meadows

Mount Dana

Tuolumne Meadows

Mount Hoffmann

Polly Dome

Mammoth Peak

Mono Pass

Pywiak Dome

Kuna Crest

Tenaya Lake

Nelson Lake

Cathedral Range

Glacier Point

Tenaya Creek

Vogelsang Lake

Yosemite Falls

Clouds Rest

El Capitan

Yosemite Valley

Half Dome
Liberty Cap

Mount Maclure

Big Meadow

Merced River

Merced River

Mount Lyell

Cathedral Spires

Nevada Fall

El Portal

Mount Starr King

Bridalveil Fall

Vernal Fall

Sentinel Rock

Clark Range

Hart Lake

Horse Ridge

Buena Vista Ridge

Chilnualna Fall

Wawona

Mariposa Grove of
Giant Sequoias

Author George Wuerthner with his daughter Summer

About the Author

Driven by a life-long love of the outdoors, George Wuerthner explores the wilderness of the United States as a full-time freelance writer, photographer, and ecologist.

He is the author of twenty-three books, including natural history guides to national parks; guides to the Sierra Nevada and other California wilderness areas; and geographical overviews of other specific regions. His writing has appeared in such magazines as *Wilderness, Pacific Discovery, Sierra, Arizona Highways,* and others.

His photographs have been featured in such magazines as *National Geographic* and *Arizona Highways,* as well as calendars and books. They also have been displayed as part of exhibits at the Smithsonian, the National Museum of Natural History, and several other museums.

He lives in Oregon.